£17·25

instant
art

k One

…ntained in this book are original and
…Le Tissier & Graphic Books International Ltd.,
…ereby granted permission to reproduce
…ed herein for general advertising and
…ne of the art is used in part or whole in
…cial resyndication such as collections of
…ings, negatives, positives, transfers etc.
…er considers to be contrary to its own
…nd copyright.

…6250 001 X

Graphic Books International Ltd.,
P.O. Box 349
Guernsey, Channel Islands (UK).

© 1974 D. Le Tissier & Graphic Books International Ltd.

Index

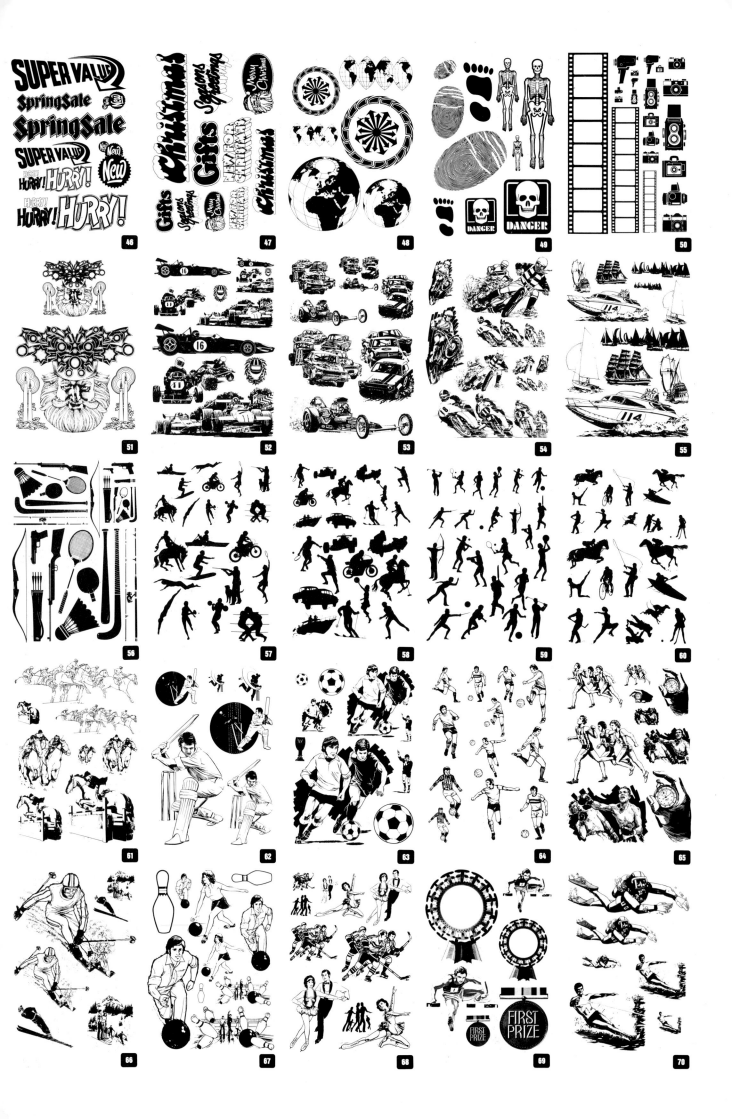

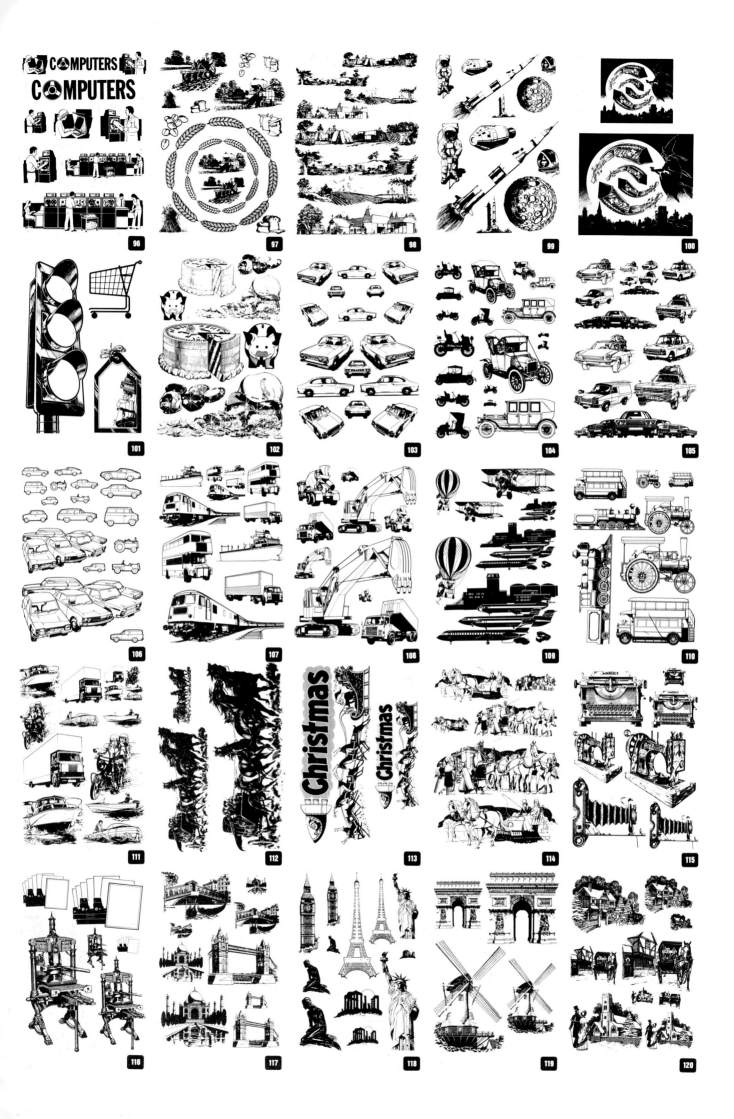

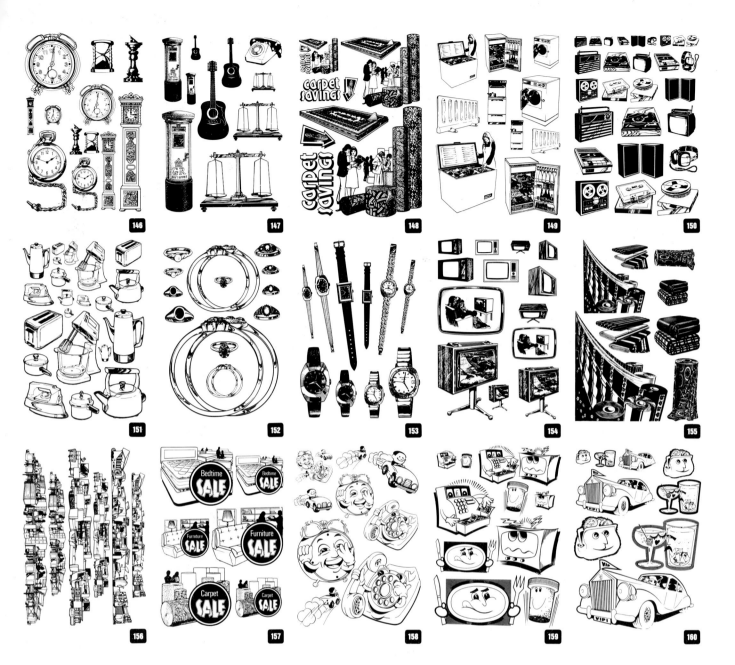

146

147

148

149

150

151

152

153

154

155

156

157

158

159

160

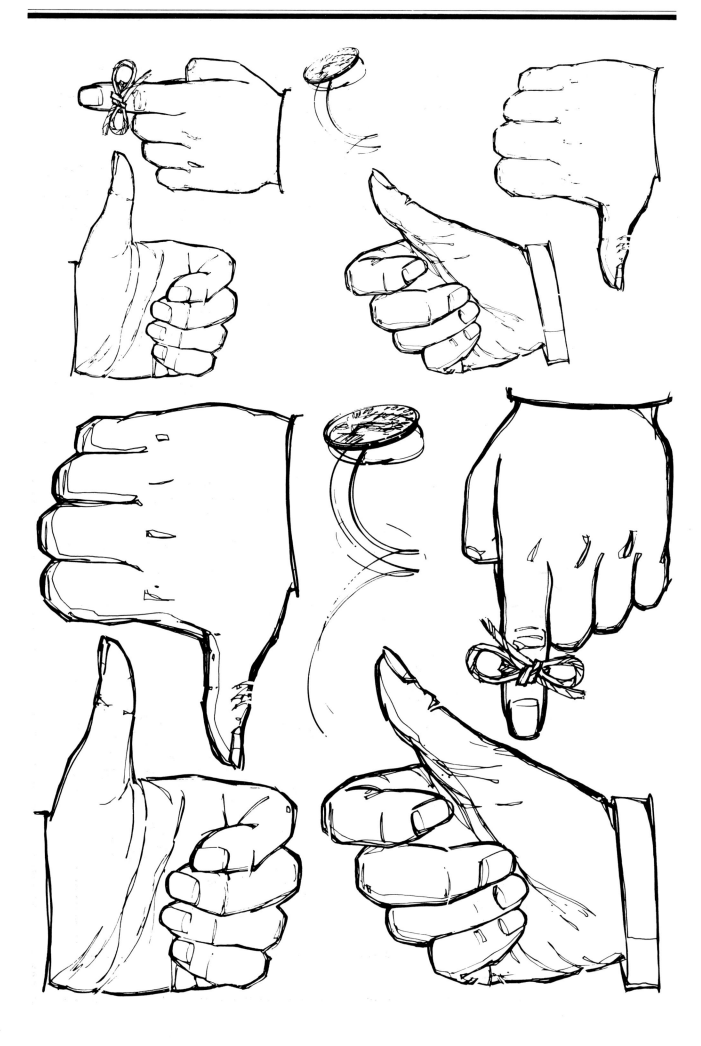

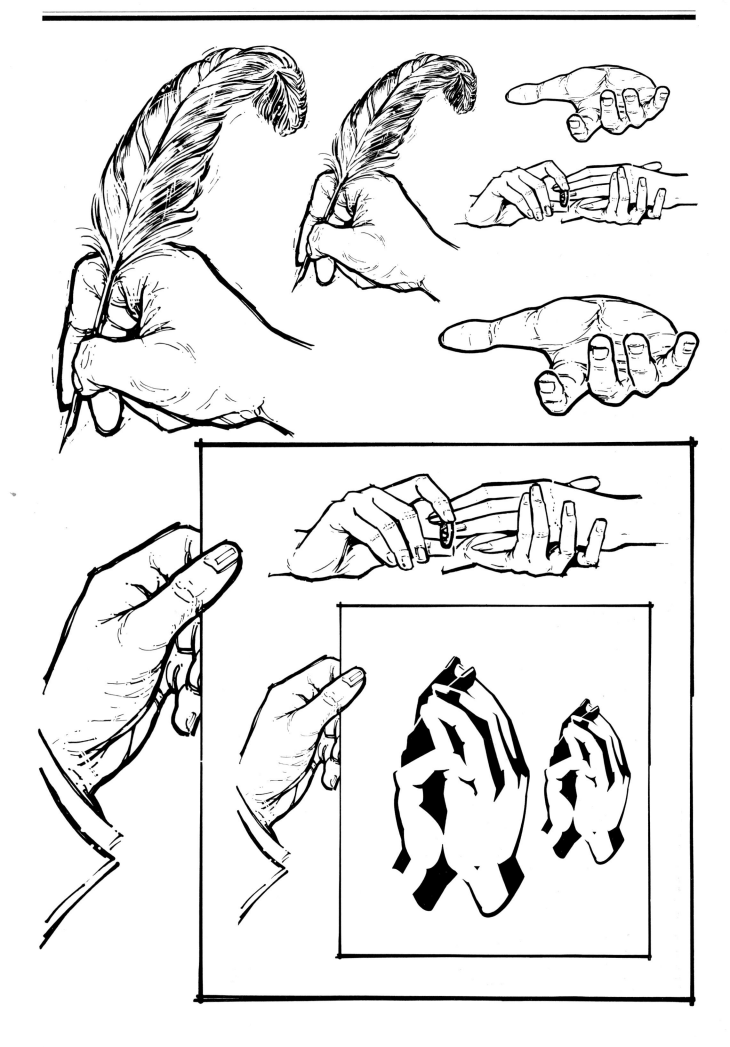

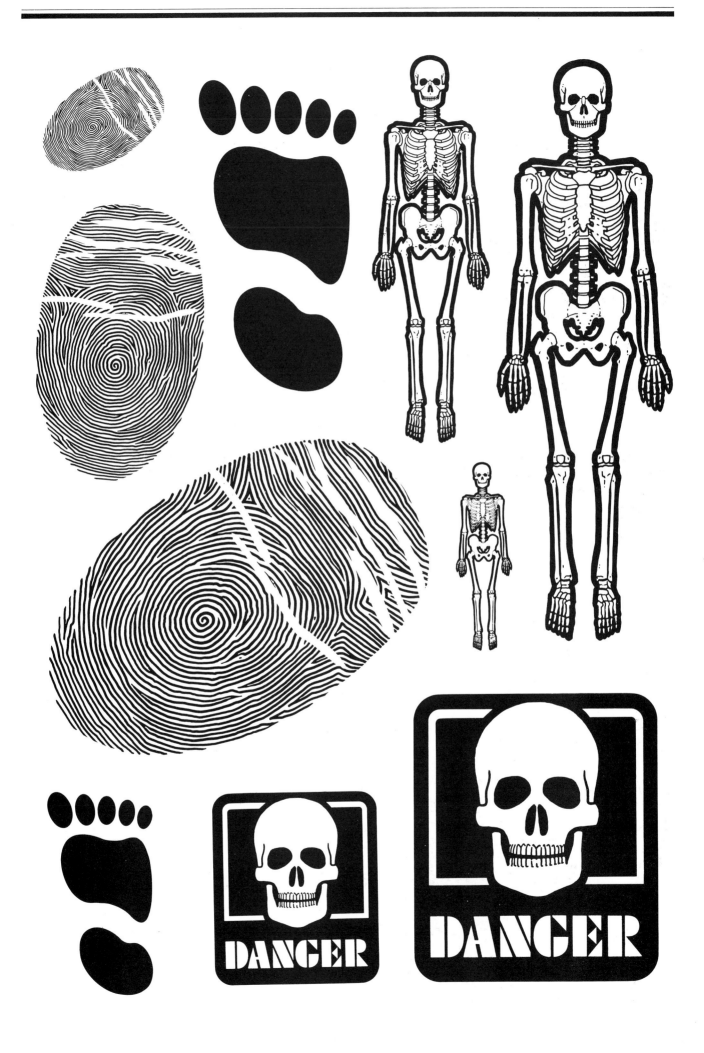

DANGER

DANGER

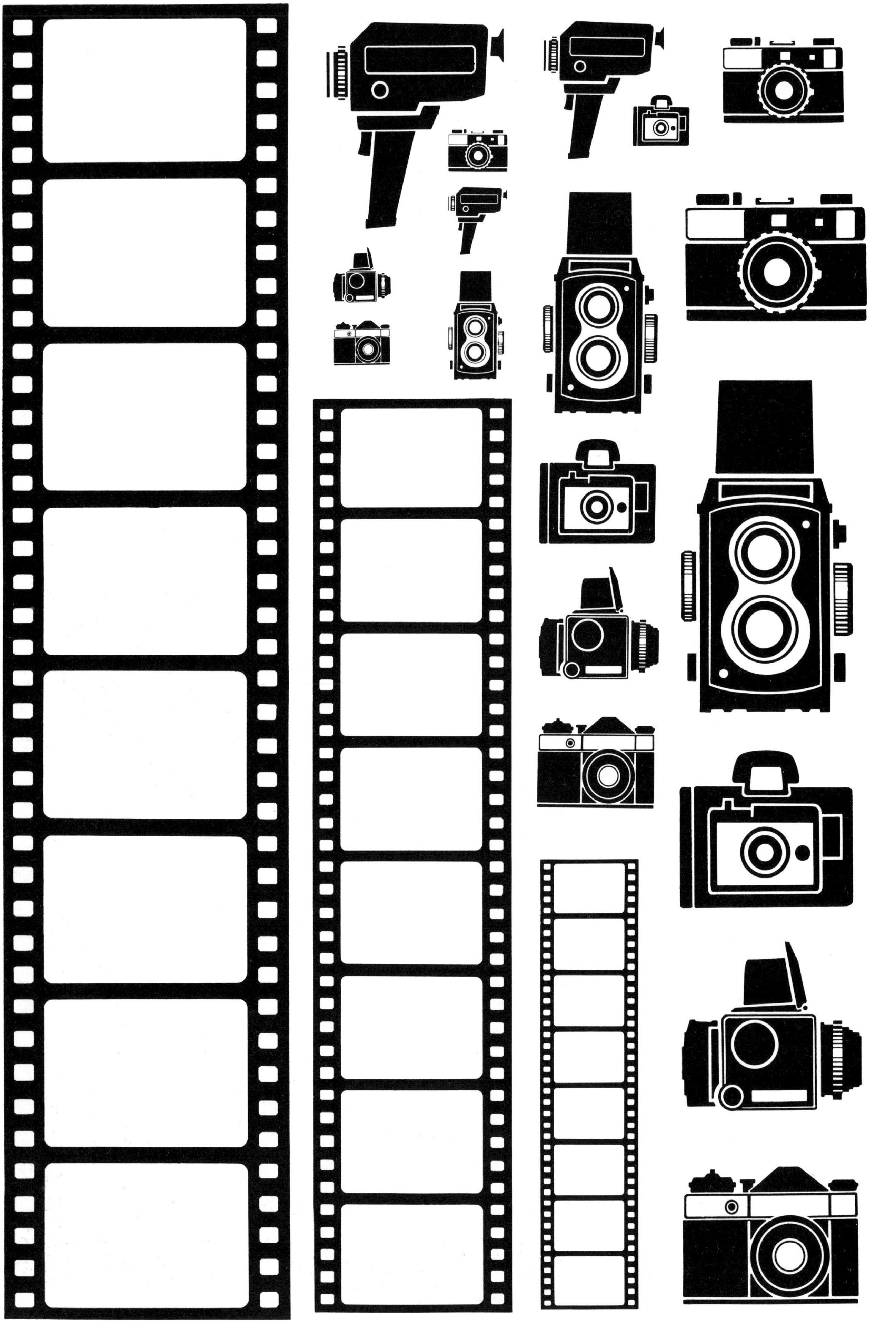

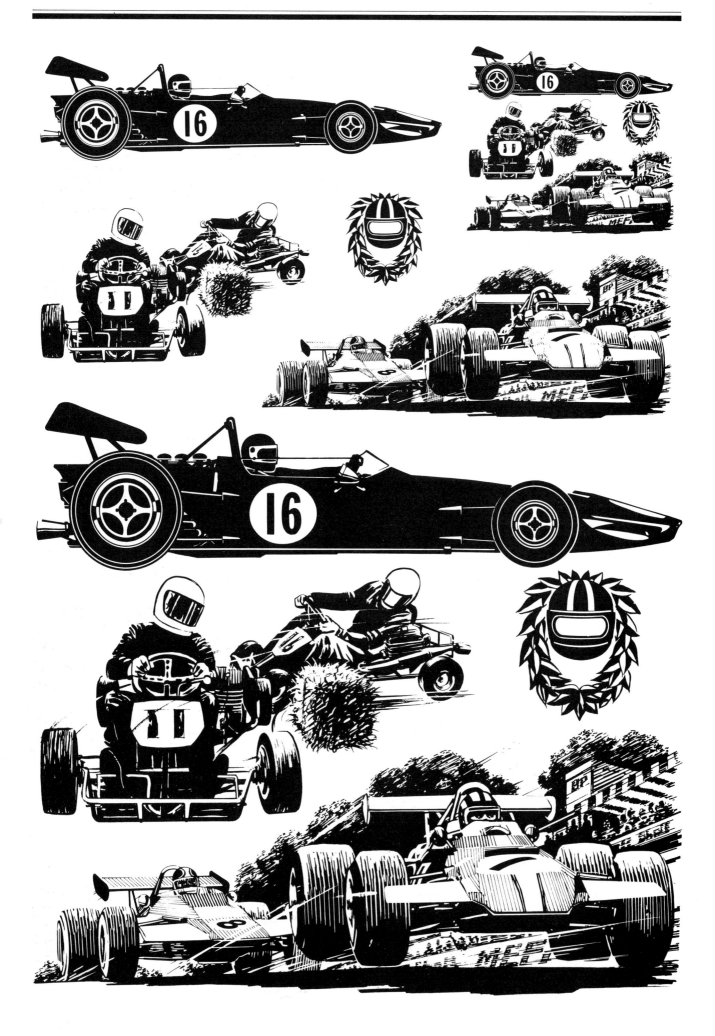

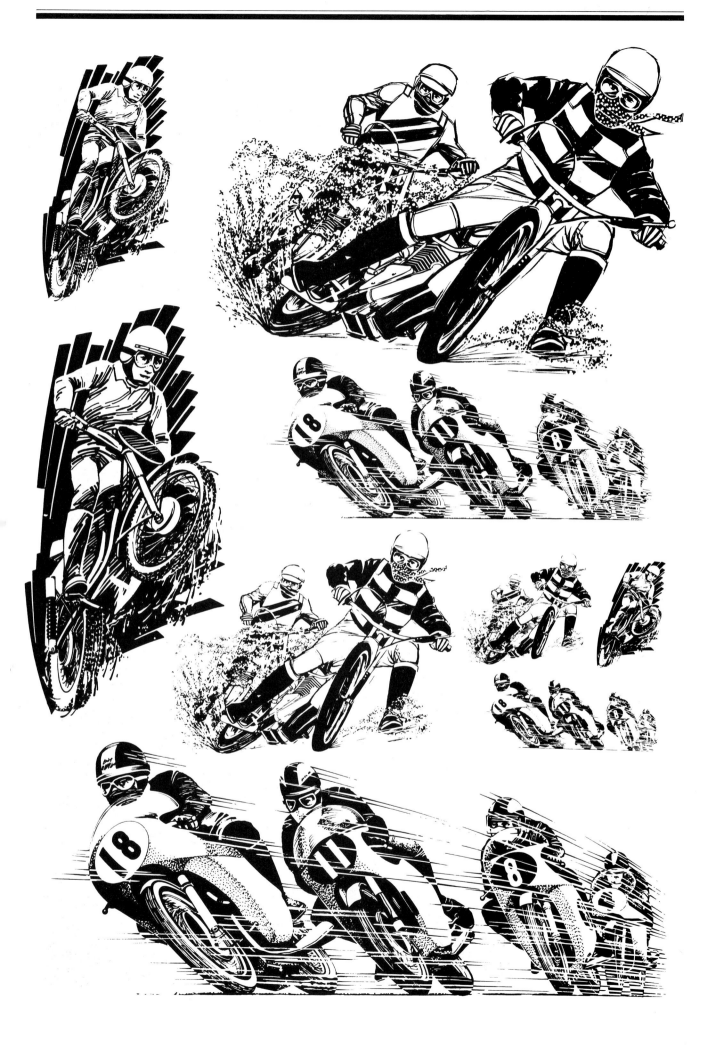

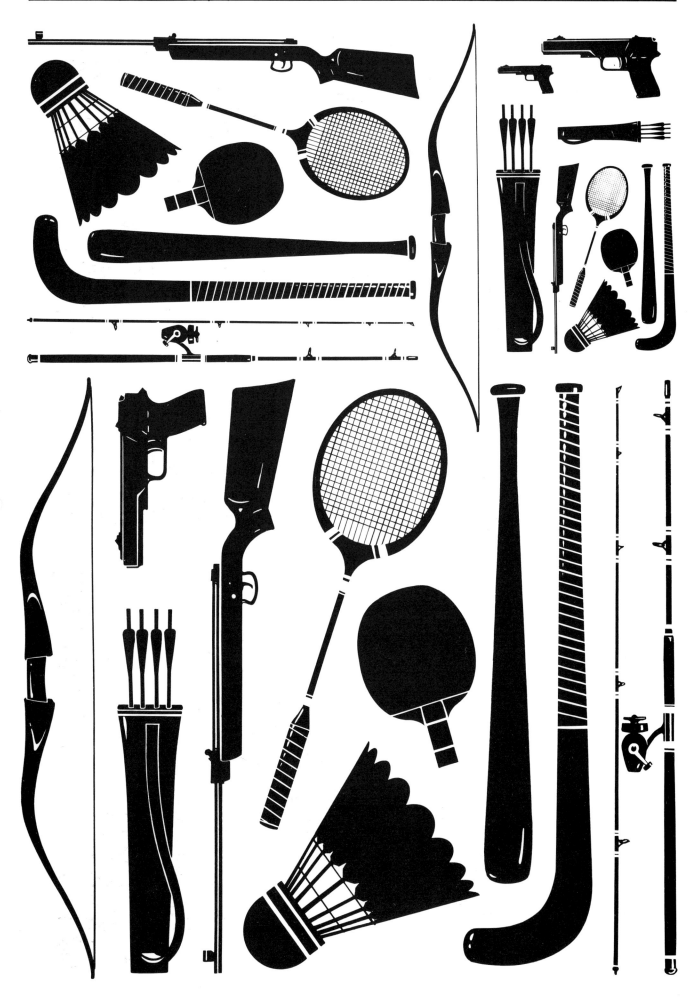

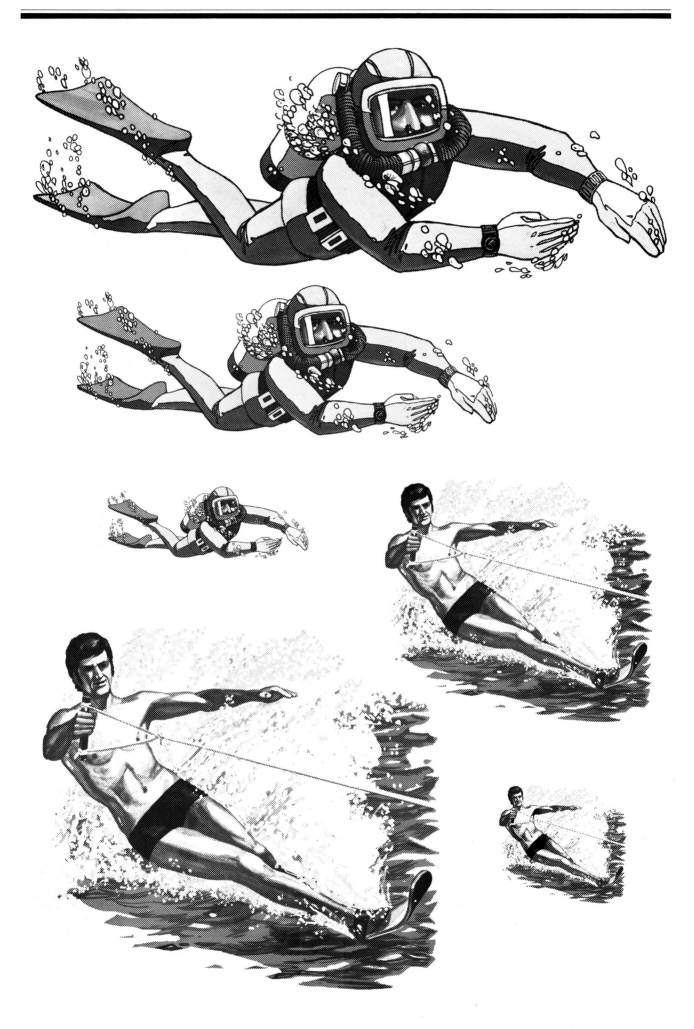

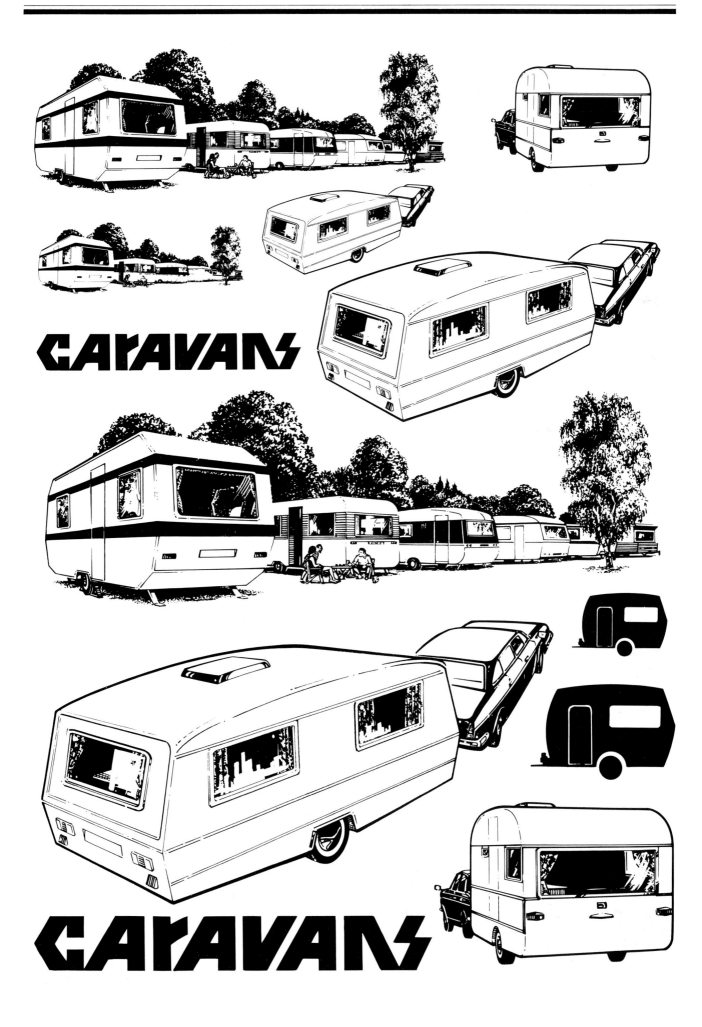

CARAVANS

CARAVANS

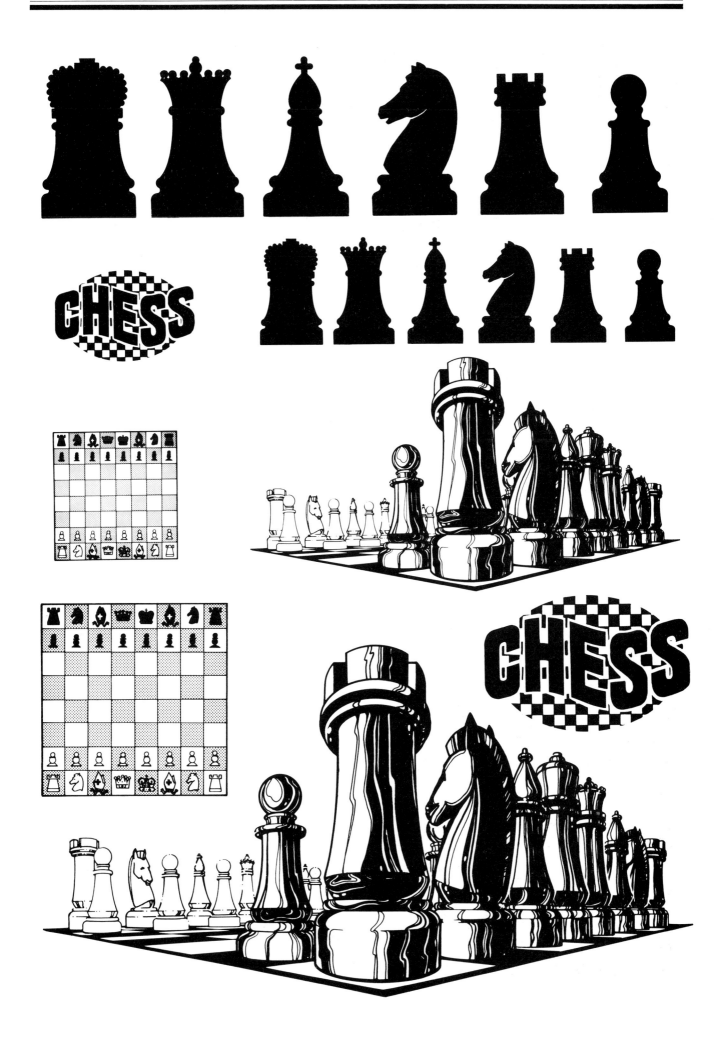

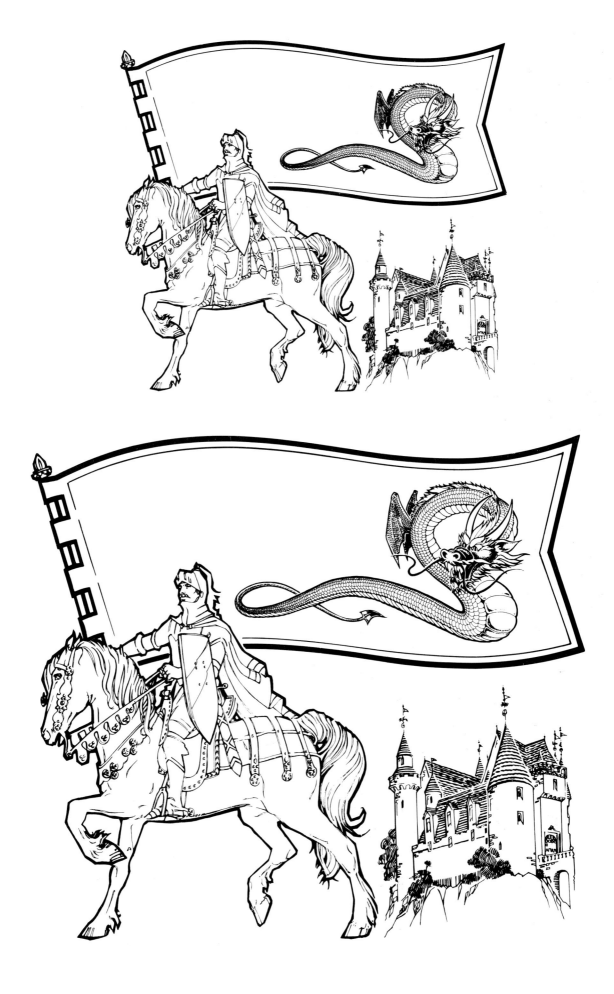

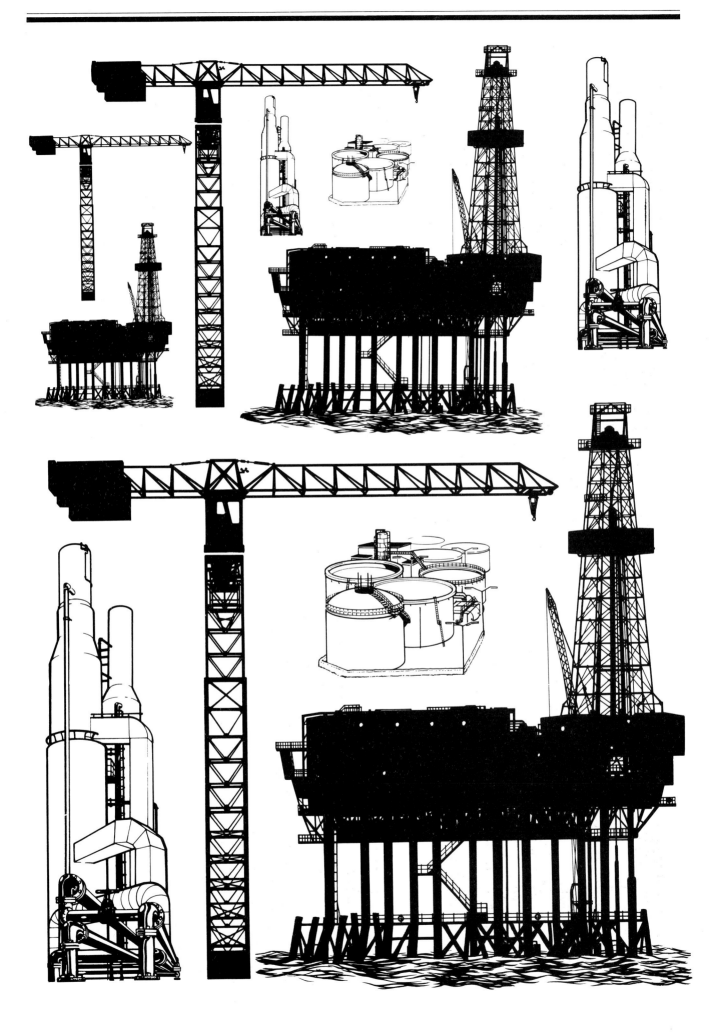

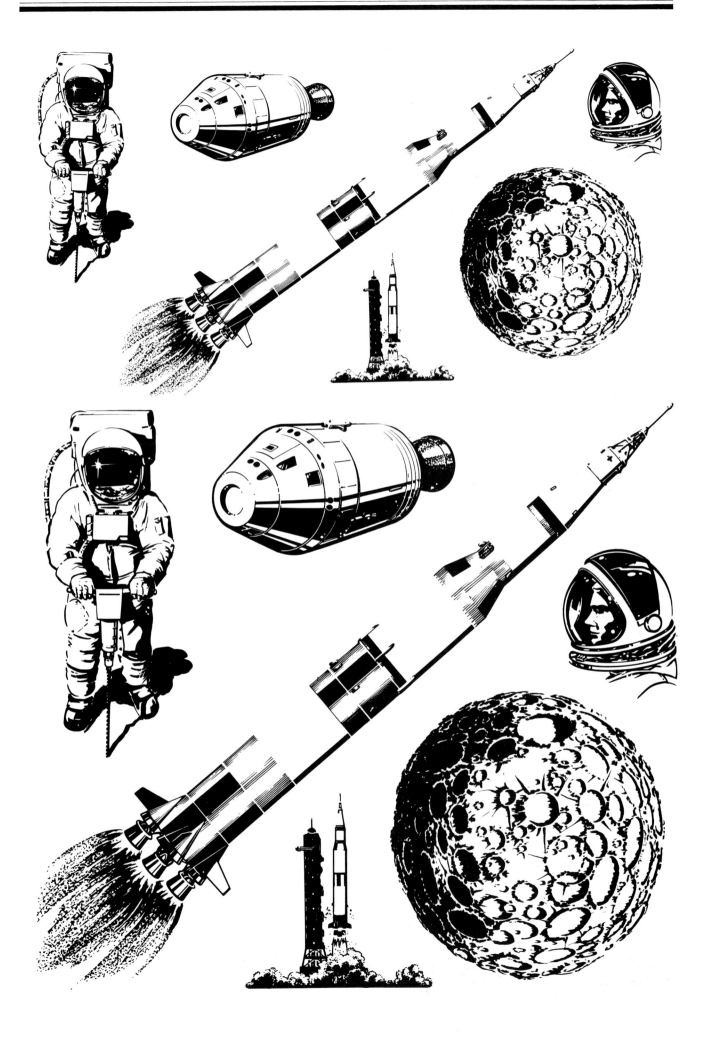

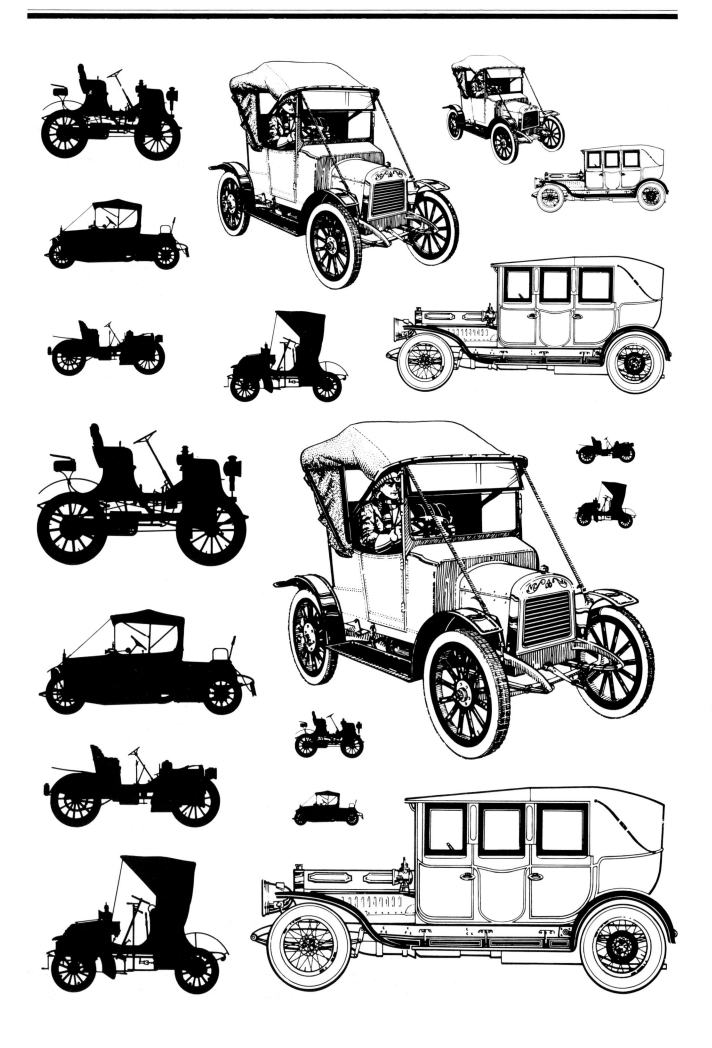

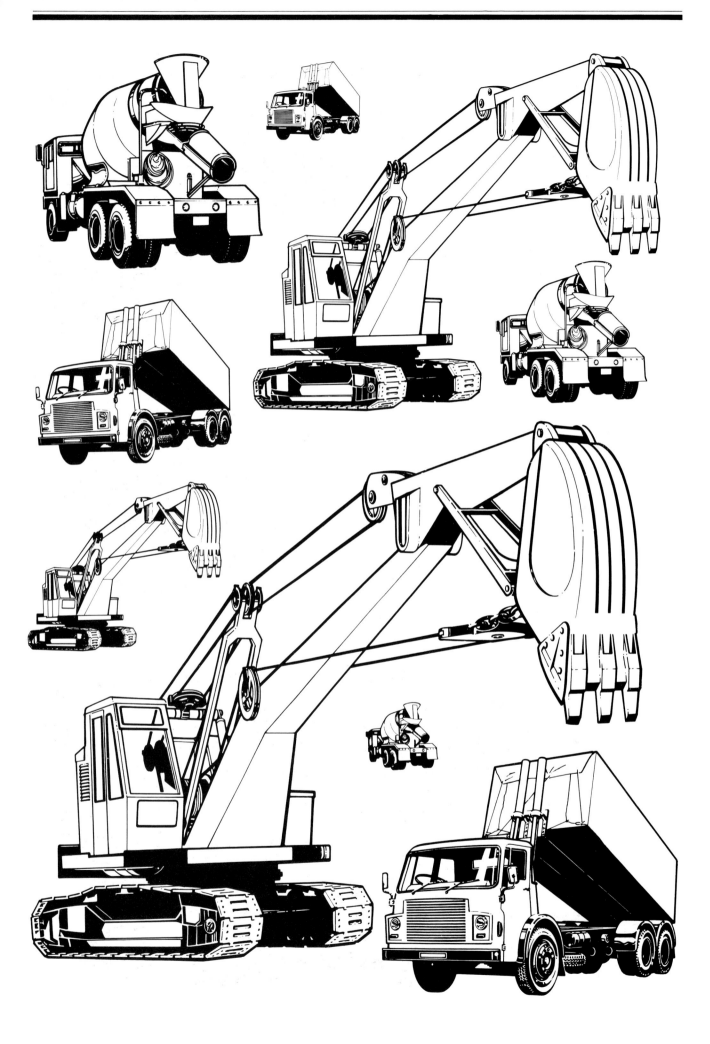

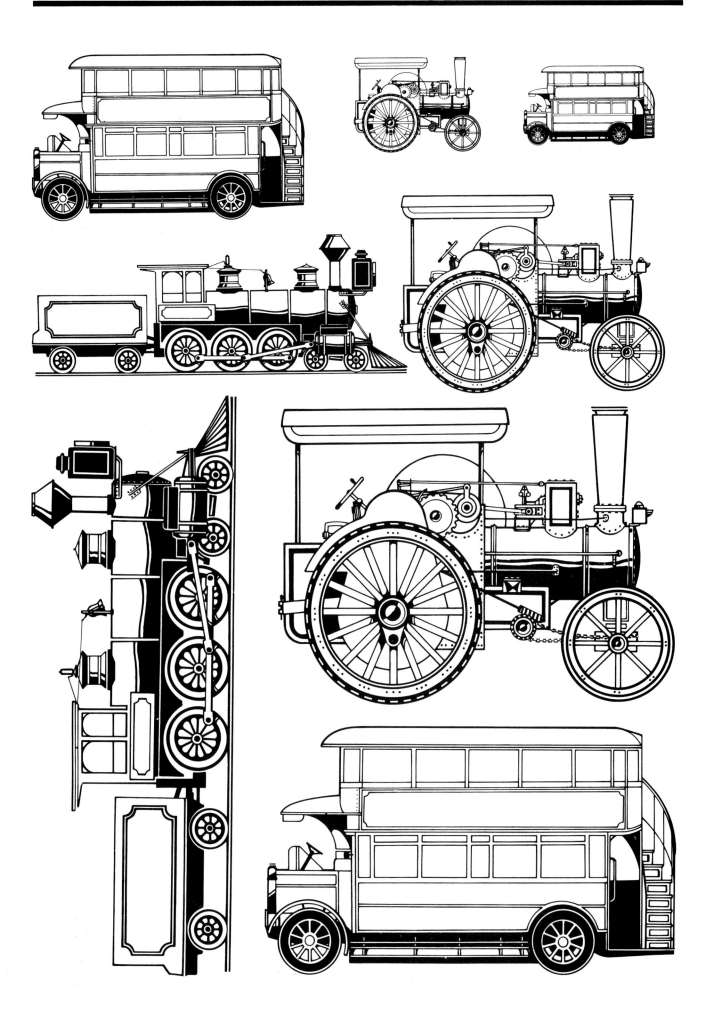

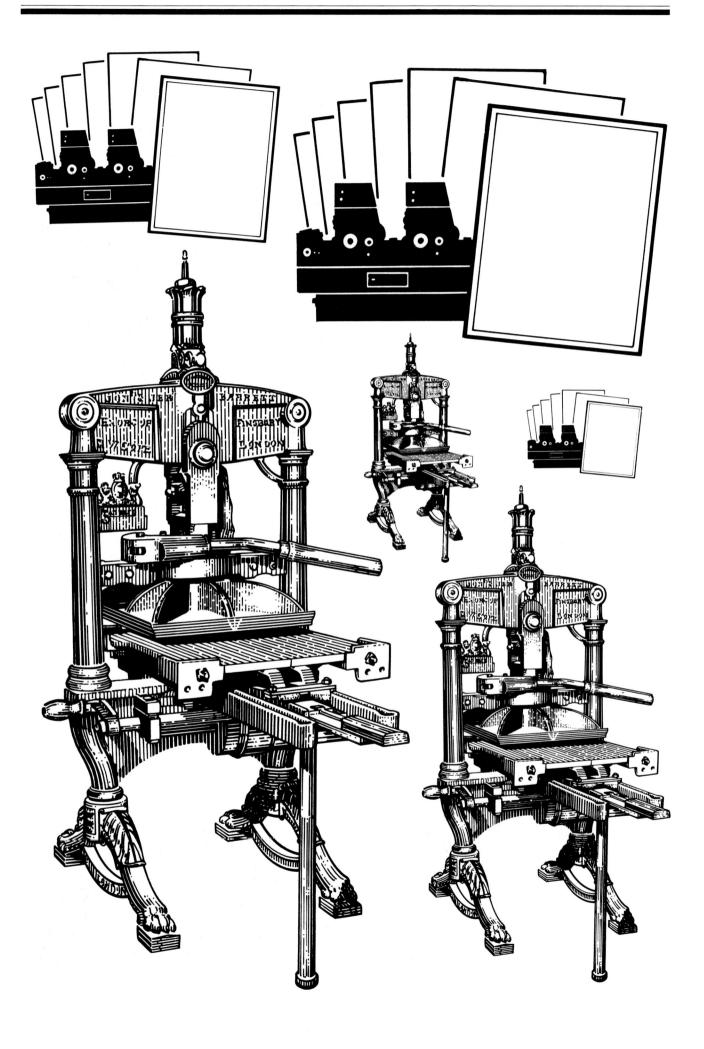

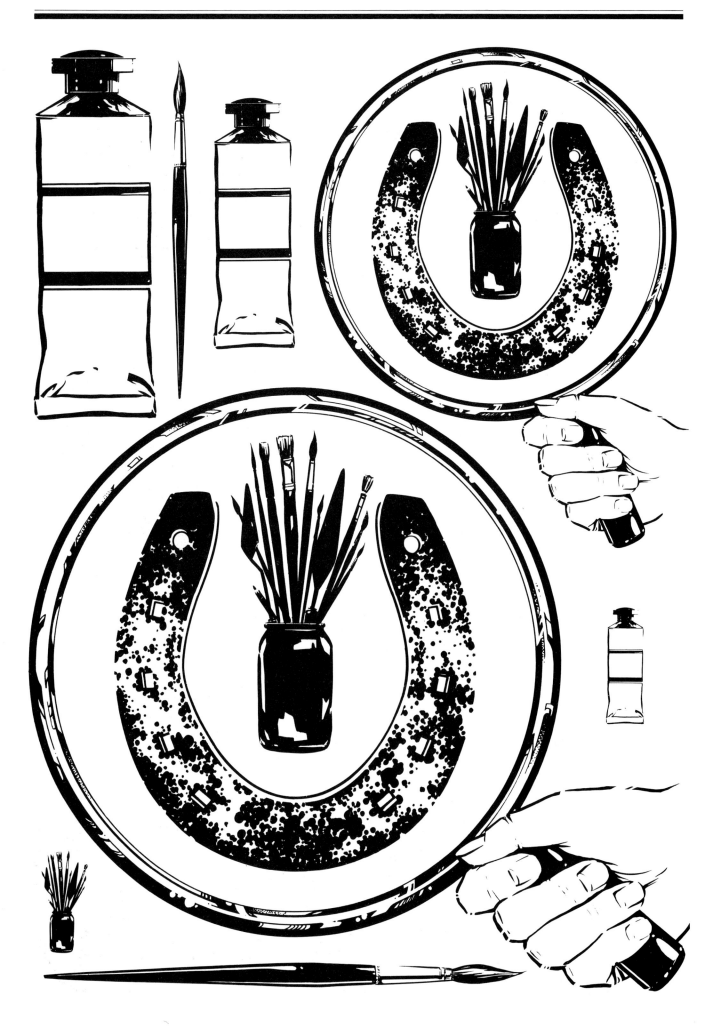

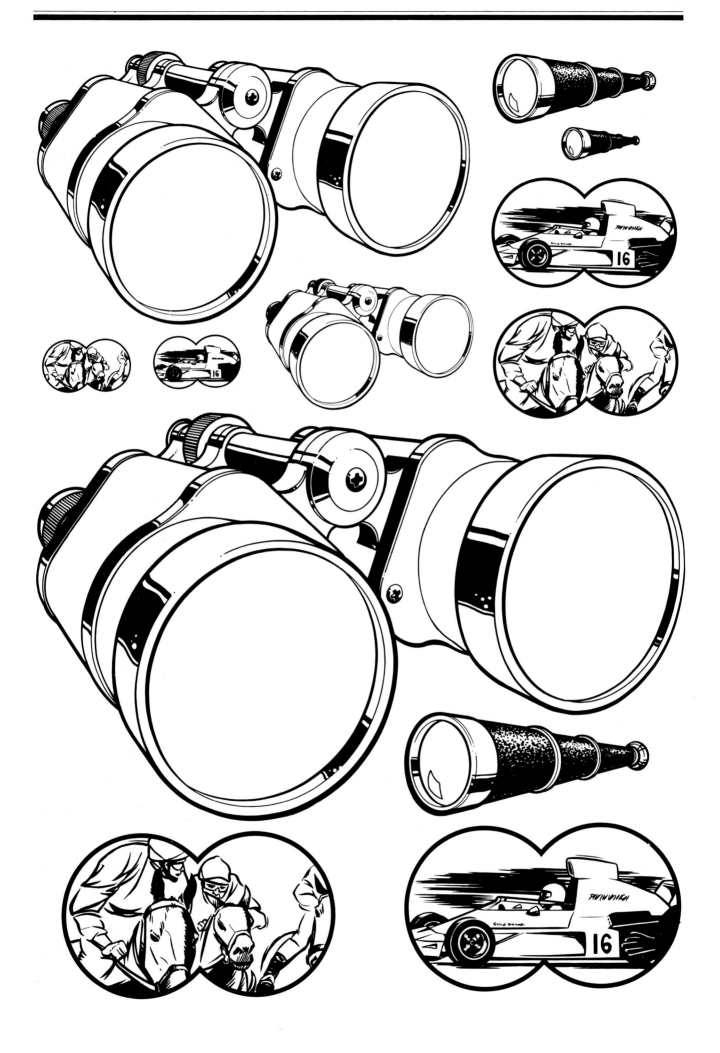

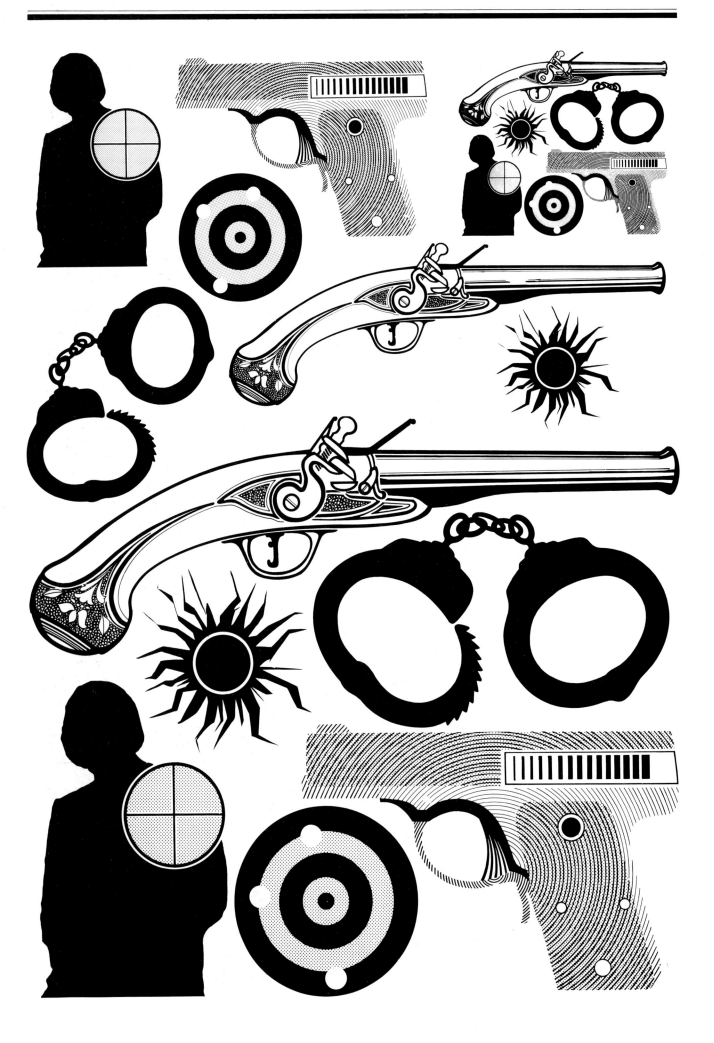

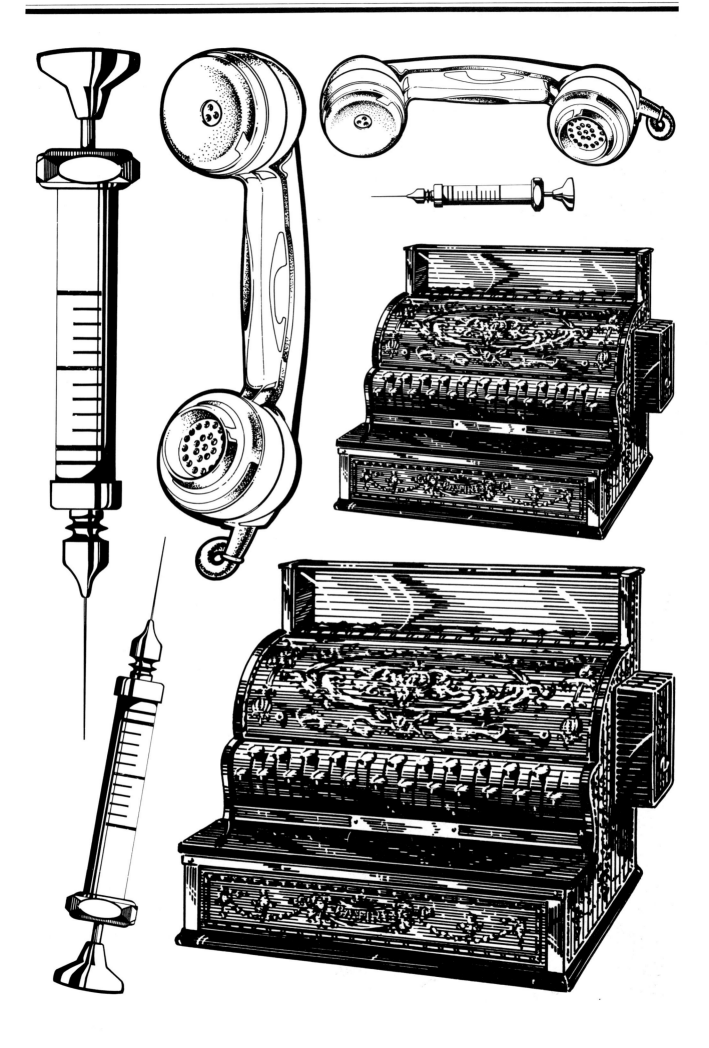

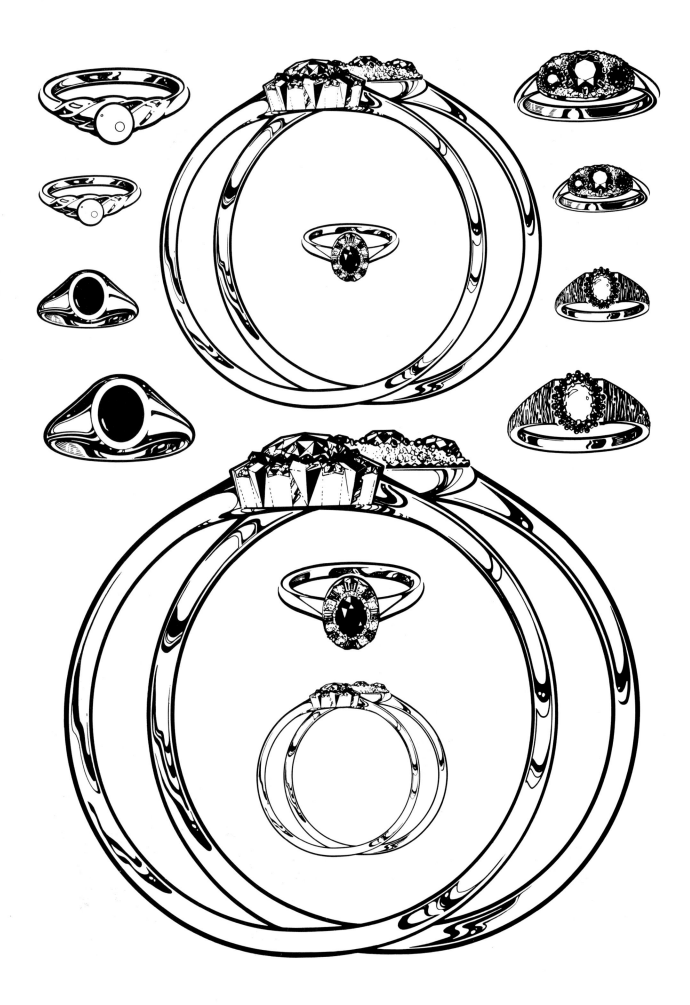

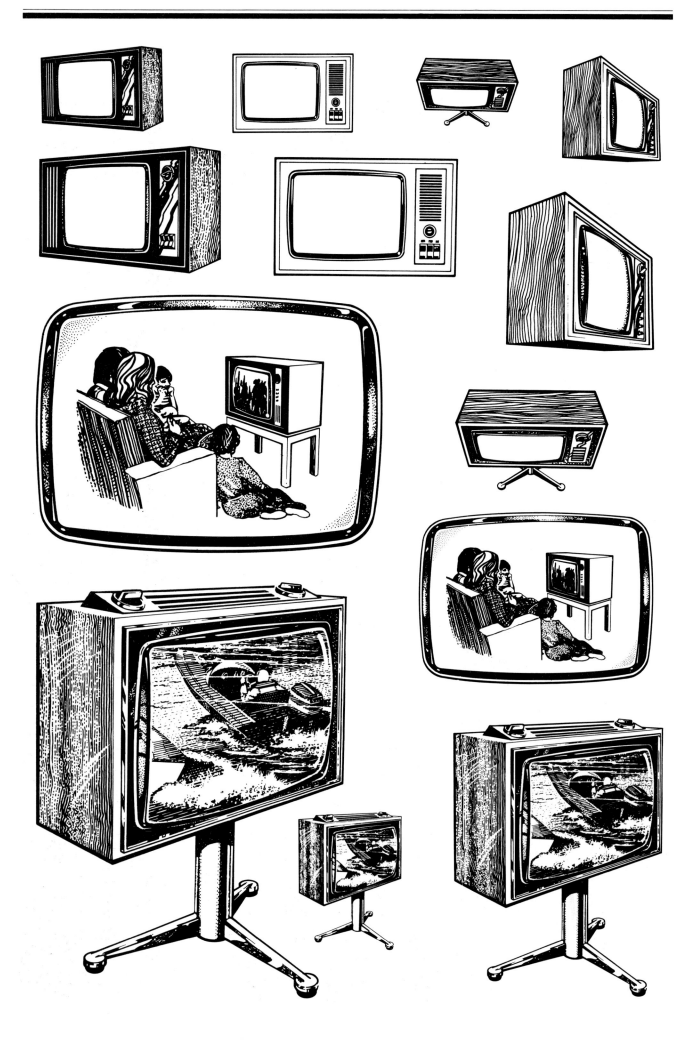

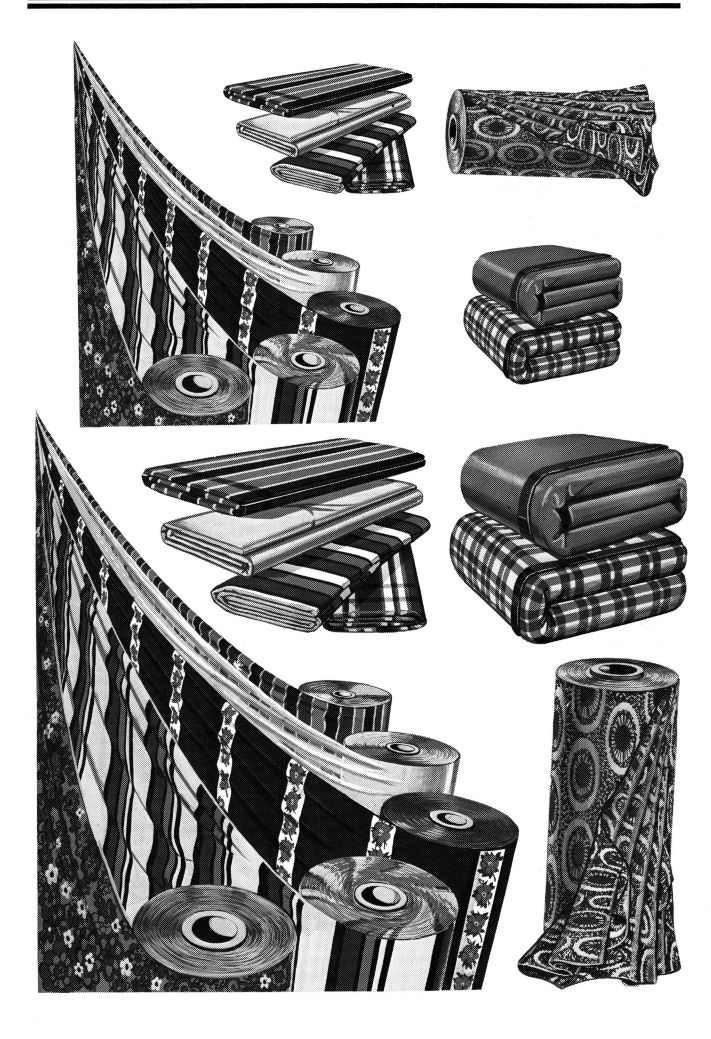

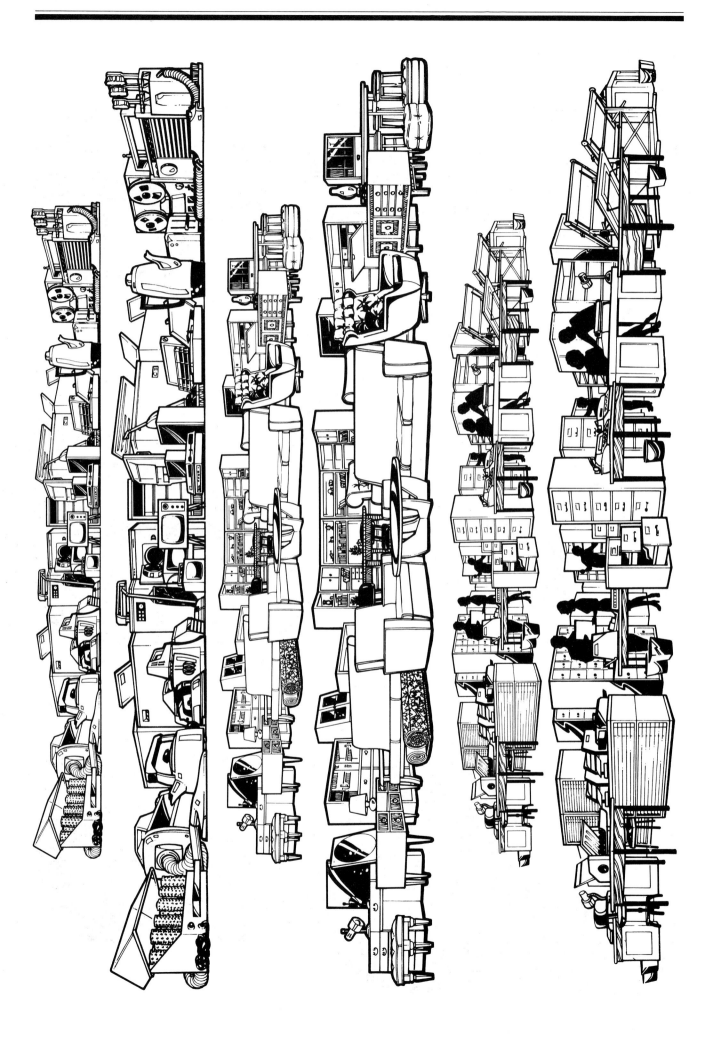